MW01264333

THE POLITICAL
MESSIAH

TRUMP *is a* **JOHN THE BAPTIST**
and **DESANTIS** *is*

THE POLITICAL
MESSIAH

JULIE SHIPOSH

The Political Messiah
Copyright © 2023 by Julie Shiposh

All rights reserved. No part of this book may be reproduced or used in any manner without written permission of the publisher except for the use of brief quotations in a book review.

Eternal Joy Publishing
Roswell, GA
www.eternaljoypublishing.com

First paperback edition August 2023

ISBN 9798218960346 (paperback)
ISBN 9798218961015 (ebook)

Cover photo: Stillfx/Adobe Stock extended license
Interior photo (Monument): Monika/Adobe Stock extended license
Interior photo (Eye of Providence): Julie Shiposh

Unless otherwise noted, Scripture quotations are taken from the NEW KING JAMES VERSION®. Copyright© 1982 by Thomas Nelson, Inc. Used by permission. All rights reserved.

Scriptures marked NLT are taken from the HOLY BIBLE, NEW LIVING TRANSLATION (NLT): Scriptures taken from the HOLY BIBLE, NEW LIVING TRANSLATION, Copyright© 1996, 2004, 2007 by Tyndale House Foundation. All rights reserved. Used by permission.

Scriptures marked NIV are taken from the NEW INTERNATIONAL VERSION (NIV): Scripture taken from THE HOLY BIBLE, NEW INTERNATIONAL VERSION®. Copyright© 1973, 1978, 1984, 2011 by Biblica, Inc.™. Used by permission of Zondervan. All rights reserves worldwide.

Scriptures marked AMP are taken from the AMPLIFIED BIBLE (AMP): Scripture taken from the AMPLIFIED® BIBLE, Copyright © 1954, 1958, 1962, 1964, 1965, 1987 by the Lockman Foundation Used by Permission.

Scriptures marked ESV are taken from the THE HOLY BIBLE, ENGLISH STANDARD VERSION (ESV): Scriptures taken from THE HOLY BIBLE, ENGLISH STANDARD VERSION ® Copyright© 2001 by Crossway, a publishing ministry of Good News Publishers. Used by permission.

The information presented in this book includes the opinions of Julie Shiposh. No claims or guarantees are made. Readers are encouraged to use their own judgment and seek out additional resources to make their own decisions.

For my husband and three daughters,
thank you for believing.

CONTENTS

Prologue ix

Introduction xiii

1 The Nation's Miraculous Founding 1

2 Trump and DeSantis 15

3 Transition from Moses to Joshua 21

4 Rebuilding Culture in Government 29

5 Cleaning House 35

6 Political Leaven 41

7 The Messenger, John the Baptist 45

8 The Political Messiah 55

9 Reclaiming the Promised Land 67

Endnotes 72

Bibliography 78

PROLOGUE

I sometimes have dreams that are predictive of future events. I have noticed that especially before significant events in my life, I will have a dream or several dreams. Sometimes these future predicting dreams are literal, and sometimes they are figurative and need interpreting.

For example, many years ago my daughter had a life-threatening seizure. Months before the incident, I had several symbolic warning dreams of impending destruction. Then two days before the seizure, I had a premonition to refresh my CPR training (I had been a lifeguard and swim instructor in my younger days). I listened to the gentle nudging and went online to review the updated CPR procedures. I thought maybe I was being prompted to do this because I had been around some kids at a pool that day and might need to keep them safe in the future. I had no idea that two days later my daughter would go into cardiac arrest and I would immediately need to give her chest compressions. By the grace of God, she has no permanent damage and ended up fully recovering.

I have also had literal dreams in which what I see in the dream occurs in the future. Sometimes it is an insignificant piece of information, and I wonder what use it was. Perhaps it was preparing me and refining my skills. Many years ago, while I was still developing this gift, I had a literal dream that my husband needed to guard the border of our property. Up until that point, I only had experienced figurative dreams and did not realize it was literal. Therefore, I assumed that it might have meant that my husband needed to guard our property spiritually by praying. It turned out that the day after the dream, an enormous Siberian husky that we had never seen on our street before came barreling through our garage and into our backyard. My husband was repairing a leaky faucet and was going back and forth from the kitchen to the detached garage. The husky came in through the open garage door and chased our pet rabbit, Kitty, until it grabbed our rabbit in its mouth and killed her. I learned to pay close attention to my dreams.

I believe this is one of many ways that God speaks to people. One of the attributes of the Holy Spirit, who lives in people who have surrendered to Jesus Christ, is the ability to tell what is to come (John 16:13). I tend to be a future-oriented person, so I earnestly seek God and ask Him to give me foreknowledge of things that are going to happen.

What does this have to do with politics?

I had a dream in October of 2021 about Ron

DeSantis and a team of workers, which I will share later in the book. At the time, I didn't think much of the dream and so just put it in my archives.

Then in early June of this year, while I was sleeping, I heard (not audibly, but I heard the phrase in my spirit), "Trump is like John the Baptist and DeSantis is a political messiah." I was surprised by this, and I started to explore what it meant. God continued to guide my understanding about this, which has since become clearer. This is the message I believe I was destined to share in this book.

You may be thinking, "Oh, she's just one of those women who don't like Trump." That is not true at all. I supported Donald Trump during his campaigns for presidency. I excitedly went to one of his rallies in Michigan, enduring the freezing rain and the thirty-seven-degree temperature. I actively participated in a car rally, standing on the side of the road holding a big Trump sign and waving at people who drove by. I happily supported him and believed he was being used by God to help our country.

Perhaps you are wondering if I live in Florida, thinking that might be why I have a message for you about Ron DeSantis being a political messiah. No, I don't live in Florida. I am an ex-Californian who now resides in Georgia.

At the beginning of this year, God led me through a season of emptying out my desires and plans for my life. I surrendered to God and asked Him to guide me as to how He wanted to use me. I was willing to let go of anything I had imagined and envisioned. After I did this, I felt a sense of peace and gratitude for small things, for the simple blessings in my life that I normally would have taken for granted. I also started to hear God more clearly as I stripped away my expectations and my plans. I began having more future-oriented dreams and sensed God's direction throughout each day. At first, I resisted the information God guided me to because I have always avoided stepping into political conversations. However, as the gentle nudging from God continued to confirm this message, I had to be obedient and share what I was hearing.

As for my background, I have a bachelor's degree in sociology from UCLA, a master's degree in marriage and family therapy from Fuller Theological Seminary, and a master's degree in education from National University. I am an author, speaker, coach, researcher, wife of twenty-two years to my wonderful husband, and mother of three precious daughters (ages seventeen, fourteen, and ten).

INTRODUCTION

Our nation, America the beautiful, has been struggling for years with hopelessness. Some people say we are under judgment from God for the evil we are committing, while others blame the divided nation and gridlocked politics. The sentiment has been that it is all downhill from here, and many people have stopped believing that our nation will ever thrive again.

That is, until Donald Trump entered the political scene. No one expected him or wanted him, but he felt drawn to politics, and he ran for president. When Trump entered politics in 2016, it was like a massive earthquake. It shattered the norm. Business as usual was out the window. In his brash style, Mr. Trump said anything he was thinking, and he would not be offended by anyone who called him out on his behavior. Rather, he commonly labeled such accusations "fake news." Initially, many people were hesitant to support Trump since he did not follow the protocol of typical politicians. At his rallies, he would talk in a casual manner, as if you were his confidant. Although he is a billionaire, he would talk like a relatable Midwest blue-collar guy.

Trump grew in popularity due to his authentic style and his hard-hitting message of making America great again and "draining the swamp." Despite being a polarizing figure, he developed a loyal following, and people still champion him through every twist and turn of his rocky path. Many people believe he had an election stolen from him and had been wrongly attacked, which strengthened even more the fury of his dedicated camp of supporters.

Trump has played a pivotal role in changing politics forever. He opened the nation's eyes to see corruption in the political system and federal agencies. No other person would likely have been this effective at reshaping politics. He brought our nation into a transformational period.

Change feels chaotic. What we used to know when we trusted our political system and government is now a distant memory. We can feel hopeless when the beliefs we used to rely on are gone. Will we ever be able to restore integrity to our political system and government institutions?

This is where we are today, in the present. We are in the in-between. We have the realization of extensive corruption in Washington, DC, but we have done little to bring justice. We feel powerless and confused about how to bring integrity back to our government.

In this book, I want to share my discoveries of

uncovering meaning in today's political climate. My sincere passions in life are understanding people and knowing and hearing God. To my surprise, it has been revealed that these skills are helpful in understanding the political problems and time period we are in.

I will be taking you through a journey of seeing God's heart for our nation and His desire to give us a hope and a future, reclaiming the Promised Land. Those who only see judgment on this nation are mistaken. An overarching message of the Bible is that mankind has turned away from God, yet God has a plan to restore and rebuild. God allows consequences for our actions, ultimately to restore us in relationship with Him. God's heart is for us, and He loves the world (John 3:16). There are millions of faithful God-honoring patriots in this country whose prayers for the nation God hears and answers.

There are only two nations in the world founded on God: the United States of America and Israel.[1] We are a nation with many problems and faults, but we have been guided and blessed by God. We have a long way to go to transform our nation, but God has not given up on us—and we should not give up either.

We are in the middle—in the middle of a comeback, in the middle of a miracle. Now is not the time to give up.

But we must understand the season we are in. We are in the wilderness. We are learning a new way of operating in politics. We will not be here forever, but how quickly we get out of it depends on us. Like the ancient Israelites, we can spend forty years complaining in the desert or we can listen to God's wisdom and reclaim the Promised Land.

The 2024 presidential election is an opportunity of a lifetime. We are ripe for change, realizing the need to "drain the swamp." Experiencing the government beast extending its tentacles of control during Covid-19 has also been eye-opening for people. We realize now more than ever the need to conquer this giant.

Our Founding Fathers had their own giant to conquer—the British, whose resources and military strength far exceeded that of the American patriots.[2] Understanding God's hand on our country's founding will help reignite our purpose as a nation. I will illustrate how faith in God and His provision was central to the principles contained in our founding documents.

Looking at the relationship between John the Baptist and Jesus, as well as the relationship between Moses and Joshua, I will provide relevant and instructive lessons for this time period in our country. I will show you how God uses different leaders for different seasons depending on the needs of the nation.

I will also touch on what is essential to clean out the culture of Washington, DC, and will share a specific dream I had that relates.

My desire in this book is to examine the country's current needs and to restore hope that God is still at work in our nation. Whether you are a believer in God or not, and no matter what political party you belong to, if any, this book is for you. I think you will appreciate the depth of insight, you will be intrigued with the analogies, and you will discover a unique opportunity in the 2024 presidential race.

1

THE NATION'S MIRACULOUS FOUNDING

I have lived, Sir, a long time, and the longer I live, the more convincing proofs I see of this truth: that God governs in the affairs of men.[3]

—BENJAMIN FRANKLIN

The United States of America has been greatly blessed and favored by God. With great favor comes tremendous responsibility to promote goodness in the world. Since its inception, our country has been a beacon of light and hope around the globe. America is a land of refuge for those valuing freedom and opportunity, who find the courage to leave their homeland in search of a new life.

We often take for granted the comfort, security, and prosperity our nation enjoys. Immigrants in America, those who have experienced crippling government tyranny and often devastating loss in their homeland, arrive here with a sense of enduring gratitude for each day in this beautiful and free country. They remember the reason they courageously left family and friends behind to make a new beginning in this land of promise. Some of the most patriotic people in America are those who know the pain of a country being destroyed by a corrupt and overstepping government.

The freedoms and opportunities we have in America were created by God-honoring patriots who risked all for liberty and justice. As described in *The Miracle of America* by Angela Kamrath, a small group of Puritans, also known as Pilgrims, came to America fleeing corruption and hypocrisy in the leadership of the Church of England. King James did not tolerate their views of wanting to purify the Church of England, and he demanded that they conform or else be driven out. The Pilgrims fled to Holland for religious freedom, spending eleven years there before departing to America.[4]

In their daring journey with other adventurers across the Atlantic Ocean in 1620, the Pilgrims saw themselves as similar to the Israelites in their exodus from Egypt, escaping enslavement. Viewing themselves as God's people, America was their "Promised Land."[5] They experienced many hardships on the path to freedom and in establishing a new way of life. Only half of those 102 passengers on the Mayflower survived the journey, and many more died during their first winter in the new land, as they were not prepared for the cold weather.[6]

The Pilgrims had a strong belief and trust in God that He would assist them in their godly endeavors. Despite encountering many obstacles and tragedies, they persevered and settled in their new land. The Mayflower Compact was written and signed in 1620 as a covenant among themselves and under God to create a civil society and to act justly.[7]

A decade later, English Puritan John Winthrop led a larger group of seven hundred Puritans from England to Plymouth, Massachusetts. This group of Puritans also desired reform in the Church of England, but such reform was not welcomed by King Charles I. They sailed across the Atlantic in eleven ships in their desire to serve God and represent Him in their new land.[8] During their journey, John Winthrop delivered his renowned sermon, "A Model of Christian Charity," inspiring godly virtues of meekness and generosity in his hearers and encouraging them to influence others in the new settlement. Winthrop emphatically declared, "For we must consider that we shall be as a city on a hill. The eyes of the people are on us."[9] Alluding to Matthew 5:14 and a city on a hill, Winthrop not only set a foundation for the Puritan settlement, but he also influenced the establishment of America's founding values as being on a mission to be the light of the world.[10]

In the early 1700s, more immigrants arrived, bringing influences from the Enlightenment in Europe. A spiritual Great Awakening was ignited, creating an emphasis on personally examining one's heart and having a religious conversion. Evangelists such as George Whitefield spoke against stale religion and called for a spiritual and moral awakening. All Christian denominations were affected and forever reformed by new spiritual influences in early America.[11]

During the Great Awakening, revivalists emphasized that man was created in God's image, and therefore each person had value and dignity. The individual was seen as having rights rather than simply being a small part of a larger community. This set the stage for the Founding Fathers to draft the Declaration of Independence in 1776, which professed unalienable individual rights endowed by the Creator.[12] Evangelist and minister Jonathan Edwards believed that God was concerned with and involved in the civil government. He asserted that the government was created to restrain the sinful nature of men and to allow people to carry out their God given purpose in life.[13]

Early American patriots deviated from the idea of the monarchical, one-man rule governance and instead favored a new form of government. For guidance, they looked to the Israelites in the Bible as a model of leadership. The Jewish people thrived under a government similar to a republic with heads of tribes, counselors, and judges. God strongly warned of the dangers of having an earthly king.[14] A motto that developed during the Revolutionary War proclaimed, "No king but King Jesus."[15]

THE AMERICAN REVOLUTION MIRACLE

Opposition grew between the colonists and the British for more than a decade preceding the Revolutionary War. The British government imposed taxes on the colonists after the French and Indian War, infuriating the colonists, who opposed taxation and refused to pay since they did not have representation in the British government. The British retaliated, and on April 19, 1775, the first shots of the American Revolution were fired at the battles at Lexington and Concord.[16]

Lasting more than eight years, the American Revolution was fought and won with a firm belief in God's provision for a righteous cause.[17] The patriots knew they were fighting against the most powerful military in the world, and they called upon God for help. Americans referred frequently to God's "Divine Providence," relying on God to guide the events of man. John Witherspoon, minister and signer of the Declaration of Independence, described "Providence" as "a firm belief of God's universal presence, and a constant attention to the influence and operation of his providence."[18] The final sentence of the Declaration of Independence declares that the patriots had a "firm reliance on the protection of divine Providence."[19] In 1781, the Continental Congress recognized God's providence and said, "At all times it is our duty to acknowledge the over-ruling providence of the great Governor of the universe, and devoutly to implore his divine favour and protection."[20]

The patriots believed that the American Revolution was won with miraculous aid from "Divine Providence." Congress declared days of fasting and thanksgiving, urging patriots to call on God's favor in helping to defeat the British. George Washington, the commander in chief of the Continental Army, should have been killed many times in battle, but he astonishingly survived to become the first president. In *The American Miracle*, Michael Medved recounts Washington's letter to his brother where he spoke of "the miraculous care of Providence." Washington said, "But by the All-Powerful Dispensations of Providence, I have been protected beyond all human probability or expectation; for I had four bullets through my coat, and two horses shot under me, yet escaped unhurt, although death was leveling my companions on every side of me."[21] The Founding Fathers considered the defeat of the powerful British military a miraculous event brought about by the hand of God.

After winning the war, representatives from each colonial state met in the Constitutional Convention. They intended to revise the Articles of Confederation, but created a new document instead.[22] On September 17, 1787, the Constitution was ratified, and a new nation was born—the United States of America.[23] The signers were amazed with the ratification, for there were many competing interests to reconcile, and it seemed at first to be an impossible task. Charles Pinckney of South Carolina described the signing as "nothing less than the superintending hand of Providence."[24] Even practical Alexander Hamilton thought it was miraculous.[25]

IN GOD WE TRUST

Understanding America's core values that were set by the Founding Fathers will help us realize that divine Providence has been and still is involved in our country. Our country was founded on faith in God and reliance on Him. We see evidence of this every day as "In God We Trust" is on our currency, in many state constitutions, on some license plates, and is the official motto of the United States.

Similar to how patriots affirmed their dependence on divine Providence during the American Revolutionary War, Americans during the Civil War were looking for a way to declare their trust in God. In November of 1861, seven months into the Civil War, Secretary of Treasury Salmon P. Chase began receiving letters from Americans urging him to put the word "God" on the currency.[26] One of the first letters he received was from Rev. M. R. Watkinson, from Ridleyville, Pennsylvania, petitioning Secretary Chase to change the design and words on the currency to reflect faith in God. In the letter, Rev. Watkinson explained that adding the words "GOD, LIBERTY, LAW," would "place us openly under the Divine protection we have personally claimed." He also suggested that the words "PERPETUAL UNION" should be inscribed in a ring, with images of a seeing eye, a crowned halo, and an American flag also added to the currency. Secretary Chase liked the idea and used some of the suggestions. He instructed James Pollack, the director of the Philadelphia Mint, to design sample coins to present for congressional approval. Secretary Chase explained to Pollack the reason for the changes on the coins, stating, "No nation can be strong except in the strength of God, or safe except in His defense. The trust of our people in God should be declared on our national coins." Upon reviewing the coins Pollack drafted, Secretary Chase asked him to change "Our God and Our Country" to "In God We Trust." Congress passed the Coinage Act on April 22, 1864, approving the new design for one and two-cent coins.[27] Then in July of 1955, Congress approved "In God We Trust" to be added to all US currency.[28]

Eye of Providence on back of one dollar bill

EYE OF PROVIDENCE

Another symbol that shows our country's foundation on God is the Eye of Providence, also called the All-Seeing Eye of God. It is an image representing God's omnipresence—being always present everywhere and at all times, and involved in the world. In 1776, the designing of the Great Seal of the United States of America began, and it included the Eye of Providence on the back of the seal on top of the pyramid. Circling the eye are rays of light, symbolizing the light of God and divine Providence shining down on the nation.[29] Above the eye are the Latin words "Annuit Coeptis," meaning "He [God] has favored our undertakings."[30] These words profess gratitude and a firm belief in God's provision. The Eye of Providence is seen in the Great Seal of the United States and on the back of the one-dollar bill.

National Monument to the Forefathers in Plymouth, MA

NATIONAL MONUMENT TO THE FOREFATHERS

America's foundation on God is clearly seen in the National Monument to the Forefathers. The monument was erected in Plymouth, Massachusetts, as a memorial for the sacrifices the Pilgrims made for religious and civil freedoms. Planned in 1820 and completed in 1889, the monument is eighty-one feet high and is the largest solid granite structure in the world. The monument displays foundational components to the Pilgrim's free society, which was based primarily upon their faith in God.[31]

The structure has one tall statue in the center and four smaller statues around it, as well as objects and images that were of importance to the Pilgrims. The tall figure, Faith, stands in the center of the monument pointing to heaven with one hand and holding a Bible in the other hand. Faith was the center of the Pilgrims' lives and the impetus behind them leaving Holland. Faith was seen as the basis of a free society. Faith is holding a Bible, demonstrating that the foundation of faith in God is rooted in biblical truths. There is a star on the statue's forehead, indicating wisdom attained by reading the Bible. Faith is looking to the east toward Plymouth Harbor, as well as toward Holland and England, from where the Pilgrims journeyed.[32]

Below Faith are four statues of four figures sitting around the centerpiece. On the north side of the monument is a statue of Morality. In her left hand she is grasping the Ten Commandments. The scroll of the book of Revelation sits in her lap. Just as the Israelites were given the Ten Commandments from God as instructions on the best way to live as a society, so the Pilgrims' firm faith and moral grounding were key components of their communities. Founding Father and president George Washington concurred, saying, "Religion and morality are the central pillars of a civil society."[33] The Morality statue appears to have no eyes because they are turned internally, examining herself, which precedes external morality.[34] Our hearts need to be changed before our actions are led by right morals.

Law is the figure of the next statue, and is holding two tablets in hand. At the foundation of Law are the words "Mercy," signifying that God gives us grace, and "Justice," signifying fairness of the law. The Pilgrims' foundational laws for living civilly were based on the biblical laws.

DESPITE OUR NATION'S FLAWS, GOD HAS BEEN ACTIVELY INVOLVED IN OUR COUNTRY SINCE ITS FOUNDING.

Education is the figure of the third seated statue. She has olive branches around her head and a book in her lap. She is teaching her children morality and training them up in the way they should go. The way to have a free and moral civil society is by teaching children these principles that will carry on to the next generation.

Liberty is the figure of the fourth statue, and portrays a man who resembles a warrior. In one hand he holds broken chains that had been bound to his legs, and in his other arm he cradles a sword. The claw of a skinned lion rests on his shoulder, signifying that the tyranny of England had been defeated.

The Pilgrims had the foundational components of a free society. The National Monument to the Forefathers shows the essential pillars that uphold a nation. Faith is largely at the center, supported by Morality, Law, Education, and Liberty. These were the foundational tenets our Founding Fathers envisioned for this country.

Despite our nation's flaws, God has been actively involved in our country since its founding. In his book *The American Miracle,* Medved says, "The evidence for divine providence doesn't prove that America is perfect, but it does strongly suggest that America is no accident."[35] God's hand has been and still is on America.

2

TRUMP AND DESANTIS

It's not enough to be in the right place at the right time. You have to be the right person in the right place at the right time.[36]

—T. HARV EKER

Reforming America's monstrous government is a monumental task. It will involve many different leaders and skill sets. God has begun the process in our nation as Donald Trump disrupted a deeply entrenched political culture.

TRUMP

If there is one way to sum up what Donald Trump stood for during his 2016 campaign and presidency, it would be the phrase "drain the swamp." Trump hardwired this metaphor into the nation—there is a swamp in Washington, DC, and it needs to be drained. Over the course of his presidency, Trump tweeted this phrase more than 150 times.[37] His loud-and-clear message evoked emotions all around—from those passionately agreeing to establishment figures disdainfully scorning.

The phrase "drain the swamp" did not originate with Trump. Several other political figures have also used the phrase throughout history. It has been used since the 1800s, but more recently, Ronald Reagan, Pat Buchanan, and even Nancy Pelosi have used the saying. In its literal sense, the phrase refers to draining water out of a wetland to prevent mosquitos from swarming. In regard to politics, the intent is to root out corruption in government.[38]

Donald Trump came at a time when many Republicans were open to hearing that their party needed reform. In 2016, Trump ran against Democrat candidate Hillary Clinton, who has been involved in numerous scandals. Career politicians Bill and Hillary Clinton exemplified unethical behavior.[39] During this time, the nation hungered for authenticity and truth-telling, which Trump refreshingly brought.

Other politicians over the years have shined a light

on media bias and government corruption, but their influence was not nearly as widespread as Trump's. In his book *The Courage to Be Free*, Ron DeSantis says, "Republicans in Washington fail to effectively represent the values of the people who elect them. . . . [This] foreshadowed the nomination of Donald Trump in 2016." The political system needed a flamboyant, eccentric truth-teller who could attract the attention of a wide audience to pound in the message of corruption in government. Trump effectively shouted from the rooftop and pointed the finger at evil with catchy phrases, hand mannerisms, a raspy voice, and superfluous repetition. Finding someone who did not know what Trump stood for would be an almost impossible task.

Because of his ostentatious manner and notorious past, many people were hesitant to support such an odd candidate. In his lively and spontaneous way, however, through his personality and message, Trump gradually developed loyal followers. He was an unprecedented messenger who drew in reluctant voters and magically won them over. Trump's message came at a time when people were ready to hear.

DESANTIS

Ron DeSantis is also a man who found himself in the right place at the right time. While in a crisis and under pressure, his true character shined. A year before Covid-19, DeSantis was elected governor of Florida and was hard at work on his blueprint, bringing accountability and needed reforms. In March of 2020, when the news of Covid-19 surfaced, our country's leaders needed to decide how to respond. President Trump urged the nation to have a fifteen-day period of closures to "slow the spread" of the virus, which turned into years of lockdowns and restrictions.

DeSantis took a commonsense approach during the pandemic. As advised initially, he attempted to limit the spread of the virus with some restrictions in his state. When the predictions of career bureaucrat Anthony Fauci quickly proved to be inaccurate, DeSantis sought out additional information beyond what Fauci disclosed. While many other leaders continued to succumb to the fearmongering of Fauci, DeSantis risked his reputation and stood up for the freedom of his people, easing restrictions based on data not just from the United States, but also from other countries.[40]

Due to his courageous leadership, he gained attention nationally and internationally for his willingness to stand up to government tyranny. He was chastised by the media, but many others thanked him for his courage to stand up to bureaucrats such as Fauci. DeSantis made tough decisions that most leaders in the nation were not brave enough to make. He was willing to go against the grain and follow wisdom rather than hype.[41]

After the summer of 2020, other leaders began looking to Florida for guidance on decisions since

Florida had better outcomes than other states that were locked down. Making the bold decision to stand for freedom paid off, and he developed loyal followers. In fact, Florida has had a large migration of people moving into the state because of his honorable leadership. DeSantis realized, "When you do the right thing, . . . people appreciate you. They know when you stood up for them, when it is not easy and you do it. That's when they go to war for you."[42]

DESANTIS MADE TOUGH DECISIONS THAT MOST LEADERS IN THE NATION WERE NOT BRAVE ENOUGH TO MAKE.

In 2022, DeSantis's hard work in Florida was recognized by his people, and he was reelected as governor by an overwhelming record-setting majority.

Ron DeSantis is hard-working and honest, and he accomplishes what he sets out to do. His personality is not what necessarily stands out to people, as it is in Trump's case. Trump's flamboyant personality and unique way of communicating has drawn attention to his timely message of draining the swamp. On the other hand, DeSantis's bold actions have been his claim to fame, as people in our nation and around the world have acknowledged his brave and wise leadership.

3

TRANSITION FROM MOSES TO JOSHUA

For everything there is a season.

—ECCLESIASTES 3:1

When skills are aligned with the right time period, leaders can be tremendously successful in their goals. Leaders have different abilities and styles. Matching the leader's skill set to what is needed for a specific time is imperative in order to be effective. In the Bible, Moses and Joshua are examples of leaders with different styles who were appointed for different seasons.

In Exodus 3, the Israelites were in slavery in Egypt when God told Moses to tell Pharaoh to let His people go. Soon after that, Moses led the Israelites into the wilderness to set up camp and wait for God's instruction. They wandered in the wilderness for forty years until God allowed them to enter the land that He had promised.

Why did they spend forty years in the desert? After spending four hundred years as slaves, the Jewish people needed to develop a new identity as a nation before entering their new land.[43] To possess their promised land, they would need to conquer giants who were living there. The lifestyle of enslavement and being the lowest in society had become familiar to them in Egypt, and they were not prepared for the battles ahead. They spent four hundred years living in Egypt—in a culture and land that were not their own. As slaves, they did not have freedom to make choices or follow their own customs and desires. The Israelites needed to learn and grow in the wilderness.[44]

The transition time was important for the Jewish people to develop as a nation and receive foundational tenets of their faith (Exodus 20–21). They were learning to rely on God and to trust Him. Throughout the wilderness, God led the Israelites by a cloud and pillar of fire (Exodus 13:21). He also provided daily "manna" as food to eat (Exodus 16). They were learning a new way of operating as free people and were completely reliant on God's provision.

MOSES'S PARALLEL TO TRUMP

Moses is a picture of Donald Trump. Just as Moses led the Israelites out of enslavement, so Trump led the nation, primarily Republicans, out of the chains of establishment orthodoxy. For decades, Republicans and Democrats have operated in a similar way, turning a blind eye to deception and corruption. Through Trump's brilliant messaging, he came with a wrecking ball to traditional politics and essentially told the establishment, "Let my people go." For the first time on a wide scale, many people realized the corruption, complacency, and self-interest in Washington, DC, among both political parties.

During the Biden presidency, Trump still has been a major focus of attention. With Trump's help, Republicans escaped political "Egypt" but are still wandering in the wilderness learning a new identity and trying to figure out how to operate. They have been hopeless and complaining, analogous to the Israelites complaining to Moses.

LEADERSHIP TRANSITION

When the wilderness time was nearing the end and the Israelites had learned a new way of living, God said they were ready to enter the Promised Land. However, they would not be entering with Moses as their leader. Moses was 120 years old when God told him he would not be crossing the Jordan River to enter the land (Deuteronomy 3:23–26). Since Moses specifically did not obey God, he was not able to enter the Promised Land.

How was Moses disobedient? Shortly after the Israelites escaped captivity in Egypt, they needed water in the wilderness. Exodus 17 explains that God instructed Moses to strike the rock with his staff so that water would flow out. Forty years later, the Israelites were near the Promised Land, but the water had dried up and the people were thirsty. The Israelites blamed Moses, accusing him of bringing them into the wilderness to let them die. This time, God told Moses to speak to the rock rather than to strike it in order to get water out of the rock (Numbers 20:10–13). Angrily, Moses called the Israelites rebels and struck the rock twice. Water gushed out of the rock, but the Lord then told Moses that he would not be entering the Promised Land since he did not do as instructed.

By striking the rock rather than speaking to it, Moses showed that he was not trusting God. Not only was this a poor example of leadership, but there are also deeper meanings to this passage that are explained in the Midrash (ancient Jewish commentaries). Some rabbis suggest that one reason God told Moses to strike the rock after leaving Egypt and then to speak to the rock forty years later was to demonstrate a needed change in leadership style.[45] After being enslaved for four hundred years, initially the Jewish people were not ready to enter the Promised Land. They were accustomed to following commands and strict orders. Striking the rock, which followed escaping captivity, signified harsher instruction that was needed to guide the Israelites into the wilderness. This is the type of communication they were familiar with at that time.[46]

During the forty years in the wilderness, God transformed the Jewish people. They developed a new trust in God and dissolved the slave mentality. With a newfound confidence in God, they were almost ready to possess their land. They now needed guidance and teaching rather than strict orders. They had matured and were ready to be educated, which is different from being commanded.

Depending on the situation, a person may need direct, harsher words or the person may need guidance and teaching. When people have been operating a certain way for a lengthy amount of time, they often are rigid or fixed in their mindset. They do not learn just by education or being coached. Direct and harsher words are more effective to get the person's attention because the person is likely resistant to change. In contrast, when a person is used to growing and learning, instruction or teaching is a more effective way to guide a person.[47]

Moses's brash leadership style was helpful for a season but was no longer needed. The Israelites had gone through a transformation, and now they were ready for a different type of leader. This explains a deeper reason why God transferred leadership from Moses to Joshua.

A COURAGEOUS LEADER

Joshua was the ideal person to lead the Israelites into the Promised Land. Many battles would need to be fought in order to take possession of the land God promised. Joshua was approximately thirty-five to forty years younger than Moses, and he was a courageous warrior, well-trained and prepared for battle.[48] He was a faithful leader who was action-oriented and methodical. Each day he relayed to the Jewish people the detailed plan God gave him; then they would head out to battle (Joshua 8).

Around thirty-five years earlier, Joshua and Caleb were the two spies who returned to Moses with a courageous report, saying they could defeat the giants in the Promised Land. The ten other spies who reported back were cowering in fear. They had observed the same scene, but they said the people were like giants, and they likened themselves to insignificant grasshoppers (Numbers 13:30, 33). Joshua's good report came shortly after the Israelites had emerged from slavery. At that time, Joshua would not have been a suitable leader for the Jewish people because the Israelites were not prepared for a leader with his bold faith. They needed to spend years purging themselves of a slavery mindset until they were courageous enough to enter the Promised Land with a leader such as Joshua.[49]

TRANSITION FROM TRUMP TO DESANTIS

Trump's leadership style is brash, volatile, and ostentatious. He effectively has been a bulldozer disrupting the status quo and calling corruption by name. The nation needed him in order to break free from an ironclad, indoctrinated political system and to shift away from an ignorant mindset. Now more than ever, the nation is aware that Washington, DC, is a swamp that needs to be drained. With this knowledge, it is time to enter in, prosecute those who are corrupt, and clean house. We need a new leader for this job who has a different skill set. We need a warrior like Joshua who is steadfast, has a clear blueprint, and gets things done. Ron DeSantis is the courageous Joshua. He is the one who knows how to create a plan, strategically choose quality team members, and accomplish what he says he will do.

WE NEED A WARRIOR LIKE JOSHUA WHO IS STEADFAST, HAS A CLEAR BLUEPRINT, AND GETS THINGS DONE.

Many people consider Joshua to have been the best leader of the Israelites since they experienced the most success as a nation during over twenty-five years of his leadership.[50] In the book of Joshua, God tells him seven times to be courageous. Before you conquer the corrupt giants in DC, you

27

must be led by a courageous leader. It is no accident that DeSantis's book is entitled *The Courage to Be Free*. Courage is one of the best attributes that can be used to describe DeSantis.

DeSantis's courageous leadership in Florida has been unprecedented. He courageously led his state during Covid-19, boldly standing for freedom and commonsense solutions rather than cowering to fear and complacency. He protected his state from "woke" indoctrination, brought integrity to the election system, and prosecuted corruption in government.[51] The nation needs DeSantis's skills and bold faith in order to enter the new land.

Moses fulfilled his purpose as a messenger. He helped free the Israelites from enslavement and transformed their identity. Like Moses, Trump brought a radical message and ushered in a culture shift, shattering the old way of viewing politics. Trump's mission is complete. It is now time for DeSantis, like Joshua, to lead us in reclaiming our Promised Land. He is prepared and ready for battle. He has shown in Florida that he is well equipped to lead the nation. He creates a detailed action plan and forms the right kind of team needed to conquer giants.

4

REBUILDING CULTURE
IN GOVERNMENT

Teamwork begins by building trust.[52]

—PATRICK LENCIONI

In order to reclaim the Promised Land, the leader needs to create a successful team. Trump has been an explosion of change in the political ideology, changing how we view politicians and government. As president, though, Donald Trump was not able to make drastic changes, such as removing corruption, like we had hoped.[53] Trump's leadership style was chaotic and ineffective in building a cohesive team to implement changes. In fact, according to a Brookings Institution study, his administration set records for senior level staff turnover. Trump had significantly more turnover than the last five presidents.[54] This is likely due to the tumultuous culture within his own administration, which limited his effectiveness.

Trump was the messenger, and his job was successfully accomplished. If Trump had also been destined to clean house and rebuild the structure, he would have already made strides in that direction. Trump influenced political norms, but did not have a significant impact in cleaning out and making changes to the government culture.

Culture has to do with people. Author and speaker John Maxwell explains that culture is "the most powerful factor of an organization."[55] Every organization has an invisible code of conduct or way of operating. People often are not aware of this, but unknowingly follow the protocol. Leaders set the tone of an organization with their behavior. Casting a vision is an essential part of culture change, but the vision needs to be played out every day.[56] When employees observe behaviors consistently, they will emulate them. A lofty vision can sound appealing, but it is just words on a piece of paper unless it is implemented day in and day out, which is a challenging task.

The most important leadership quality is integrity.[57]

Leaders build trust by being consistent, having the right motives, and being exceptionally honest. People intuitively sense whether or not they can trust a leader, and they will adjust their behavior accordingly. In addition, when leaders are authentic and admit when they make a mistake, they build trust and safety within the organizational culture. As honorable behavior is modeled and expected in an organization, the more prevalent it is within the system. Leaders often lack the skill of ownership and get defensive, pushing back when being called out. Defensiveness is an automatic response of a prideful posture of self-protection. They defend themselves at all costs. Unfortunately, this erodes trust, which is hard to rebuild. It can be said that trust is earned in drops, but lost in buckets. Leaders with integrity are more concerned with being transparent and building relationships with those around them than with preserving their ego.

IF TRUMP HAD ALSO BEEN DESTINED TO CLEAN HOUSE AND REBUILD THE STRUCTURE, HE WOULD HAVE ALREADY MADE STRIDES IN THAT DIRECTION.

In the Bible, even the Son of God, Jesus, had

disciples to carry out his mission. Jesus chose twelve disciples as his team, who he trained and empowered to implement the Great Commission of making disciples of all nations (Matthew 28:16-20). Over two thousand years later, their mission is still being carried out in the modern-day church.

As Governor, creating a strategic team aligned with his objectives was important to DeSantis and enabled him to execute his vision. In his book, he explains, "As an executive, one can have a great governing program, but if the individuals staffing the administration do not share in the governing vision and/or have ulterior motives, then even the best-laid plans will go up in smoke."[58] As president, he says he will focus on hiring people who have the agenda of the American people, and of his mission. Someone like Fauci, who had his own agenda, would have been terminated.[59] DeSantis has a track record of selecting effective leaders and holds people accountable.

GOVERNMENT CULTURE

A culture of corruption and lack of accountability has permeated politics and government. In *The Courage to Be Free,* Ron DeSantis recounts scandals involving the IRS, FBI, law enforcement, election protocols, etc. National trust of government is at a near all-time low. According to the Pew Research Center, as of May 2022, only 20 percent of Americans have trust in government.[60] Only 26 percent of those who lean heavily Democrat trust government, and only 9 percent of the most conservative Republicans have trust in government. Since 2007, the average trust in government has not been higher than 30 percent. Reform and culture change is needed now more than ever.

Trump was a talented leader in many ways and exposed the darkness of the DC swamp. He served his purpose in a way our nation needed, but he is not a culture rebuilder—he is a culture disrupter. The government and political arena need an overhaul. We simply cannot just drain the swamp; we need to clean it out and rebuild it.

Holding officials accountable is a critical aspect of government overhaul that has not been thoroughly done, degrading trust in federal institutions. Partisan politics and corrupt leaders have contributed to many government crimes. To restore trust, a leader needs to hold people accountable to the law, no matter what political party the person represents.

Reestablishing integrity in our government is a major undertaking and needs to be strategically done by the right leaders. Virtuous culture in our institutions is not developed through fearmongering or threatening termination for any reason. These leadership behaviors lead to distrust and a lack of transparency, causing employees to hide and conceal matters rather than bring them into the light.

The government will be transformed by an honorable leader who creates a team with a vision and detailed action plan, methodically carrying out the mission. By modeling virtuous leadership and holding people accountable, a leader will shift the culture and begin to establish trust in institutions. For America to continue being a beacon of light to the world, we need to reestablish integrity in the government.

5

CLEANING HOUSE

The world is a dangerous place to live; not because of the people who are evil, but because of the people who don't do anything about it.[61]

—ALBERT EINSTEIN

The Jewish holiday of the Feast of Unleavened Bread provides insight regarding cleaning out corruption in politics. The weeklong festival is a time to remember how God suddenly brought the Israelites out of slavery. People prepare for weeks to get ready for the festival.

The day before the Feast of Unleavened Bread is the Passover holiday. After the temple was built, the

Israelites would pilgrimage to Jerusalem for ceremonies in the temple. The Passover is a meal celebrating and remembering how God brought the Jewish people out of slavery. God told Moses to tell Pharoah, "Let my people go" (Exodus 5:1; 9:1). Moses agreed and obeyed God. Initially, Pharoah resisted, as he would lose about a million hardworking slaves. God then sent ten plagues upon Egypt (Exodus 7:14-12:36). Before the last plague, the Jewish people were instructed to put the blood of a lamb or goat on their doorpost so that God would pass over their house and not put their firstborn to death. They followed these orders, and then destruction came upon Egypt at midnight.

Devastated from the massacre, the Egyptians pleaded with the Israelites to leave their land so they would be saved from complete extinction. When the Lord said it was time, the Israelites urgently fled Egypt, grabbing their bread, which was still unleavened (without a rising agent) in kneading bowls. After Passover comes the weeklong Feast of Unleavened Bread, when Jewish people abstain from eating or possessing anything that has "chametz," the Hebrew word for leaven or yeast. They are to remember how God brought them out of captivity so suddenly that they left even their leaven behind.

The Feast of Unleavened Bread requires weeks of rigorous preparation.[62] Jewish people are to clean their houses, cars, properties, clothes, and anything else they own. They get rid of any product containing leaven (yeast), even if it means selling it to someone else temporarily. After cleaning for contaminants, the checking begins. During this process, there is a thorough checking for any crumbs or remains of *chametz*. They search for any leaven under furniture, in corners or cracks, in pockets, and everywhere else. Checking for leaven is not taken lightly, and the search is meticulous. Once all the possible crumbs have been collected, they are put into a sealed bag, and the next morning the pieces are burned in a ceremony.[63]

Leaven, and the process of removing it, has an important meaning. Leaven is used to help dough rise before baking. The fermentation process causes bubbling and gassing and puffs up the dough. The rotting process, which makes the dough puffy, is similar to impurities or sin in our hearts puffing up our ego. Senior Rabbi Alan Green explains, "We absolutely need an ego to function in this world, but the problem is that it is subject to getting too big and begins to see life in terms of self instead of serving others."[64] People with puffed-up egos tend to be takers rather than givers. They focus on self-interest instead of on the interests of others.

As Rabbi Green stated, we need an ego to function in life. An ego gives us a sense of motivation, resilience, and esteem. When tempered, the ego is in a healthy state. A person will care about others, but will also address their own needs, which is necessary. The problem arises when rotting fermentation is uncurbed in the heart and impurities puff up the ego bigger and bigger. Such people are focused on themselves and their own advances instead of being focused on serving others and looking for ways to meet their needs.

In preparing for the Feast of Unleavened Bread, the purpose of thoroughly cleaning the house of leaven symbolizes cleaning out corruption in one's heart, which overly puffs up the sense of self. It is a process of humbling yourself and letting the ego deflate. Just as matzah, the unleavened bread, is flat, so the sense of self is to be humbled and flattened during this annual festival.[65]

> OUR LEADERS HAVE ABANDONED THE PRINCIPLES OF VIRTUE AND SELFLESS LIVING INSTILLED BY THE FOUNDING FATHERS.

The Bible describes the root of all evil as selfishness, pride, or coveting (wanting what others have), which are all related to a puffed-up sense of self (see Isaiah 14:13–14; Matthew 16:24; 1 Timothy 6:10; James 1:13–15). When Jesus was asked what the greatest commandment was from the Jewish Law and Prophets, His answer was about humbling yourself.[66] He said, "'You shall love the Lord your God with all your heart, with all your soul, and with all your mind.' This is the first and great commandment. And the second is like it: 'You shall love your neighbor as yourself'" (Matthew 22:37–40). Seeking God first and looking out for the interests of others are the priority. When Jesus says, "Love your neighbor as yourself," there is an assumption that we already take care of and elevate ourselves. It is human nature to seek our own interests. Our ego naturally wants to dominate our lives. We need to deflate it, elevating God and others, which is not an innate inclination. The root of corruption can be traced to a puffed-up heart that has not been scrutinized in order to clean out self-serving impurities.

Leaders such as the Founding Fathers humbly relied on God, not seeking to elevate themselves or their status, but instead sacrificing everything they had for the cause of freedom. They knew how to keep their tendency for a puffed-up sense of self in check by honoring God and serving others. This is the type of leadership God uses to conquer giants.

Washington, DC, has become an epicenter of elites with inflated egos seeking to be served rather than desiring to humbly serve others. This is the root of corruption in our government. Our leaders have abandoned the principles of virtue and selfless living instilled by the Founding Fathers. We need leaders in Washington, DC, without puffed up egos and self-serving agendas.

DREAM: RON DESANTIS "CLEANING HOUSE"

In October of 2021, I had a dream that Ron DeSantis and a crew of people charged into a house and moved out furniture. Then he shook my hand and proceeded to impeccably clean every square inch of the house. I was struck by the dream, and it seemed strange to me how thoroughly he and the crew were cleaning. At the time, I did not know what the dream meant or why I had it, so I simply wrote it down in my dream journal. Then on June 9, 2023, I heard in my spirit while I was sleeping, "Trump is a John the Baptist and DeSantis is a political messiah." The next day I started looking more into the 2021 dream, as well as the phrase I had just heard, and I unveiled what it meant. Similar to how the Jewish people prepare for the Feast of Unleavened Bread by extensively cleaning their homes and earnestly searching for any leaven, DeSantis will do this as president. The dream means: DeSantis and his team will thoroughly seek out political corruption in the government and remove it from contaminating the culture. It is time to clean house of inflated egos and corruption in Washington, DC.

6

POLITICAL LEAVEN

*If a government official lies to you, it is public service.
If you lie to them, it is a felony.*[67]

—JAMES BOVARD

The leaven in Washington, DC, has rotted uncontrolled for many years.[68] Politicians and government agencies have forgotten the principles this nation was founded on, as well as those who sacrificed so we can live in a free society. Referring to the puffed-up political elites, DeSantis said, "We are supposed to all be equal before the law, but we have a separate and distinct ruling class, and that is wrong."[69] They have neglected the virtue of being selfless representatives serving the citizens of this nation.

Since corruption has been tolerated in political agencies and has not been thoroughly prosecuted, it has infiltrated the entire system. Leaven is yeast. When yeast is added to dough, it permeates every part of it. The yeast does not stay in one part of the dough and leave the other part untouched. In the New Testament, Jesus warned His disciples, "Beware of the leaven of the Pharisees, which is hypocrisy" (Luke 12:1). The leaven, or yeast, in that verse refers to the self-importance, pride, and arrogance that the religious leaders had toward others. They knew the Jewish laws meticulously, but their hearts were full of pride and were puffed up.

The top priority for the next president will be to clean out the leaven in Washington, DC. The longer evil is tolerated in our government, the more widespread it becomes. The self-serving partisan corruption needs to be rooted out in order to restore integrity to our country's foundation.

The leader who selects a team and searches for leaven must be someone who regularly searches and cleans out his own heart. We need a tone-setter, someone who knows how to keep his own house in order as an example to others. This person would be humble, self-sacrificing, and self-controlled. The primary gifting needed for the new political season is not a messenger to point out evil, but a leader of a team (as in my dream) who will search out and find and remove the evil. With a leader who

POLITICAL LEAVEN

has the drive to set a standard of integrity and transform culture, Washington, DC, will be rebuilt and will deflate in self-importance.

The standard of politics will begin to change when led by a person whose mission is to serve rather than to inflate an ego.

As governor of Florida, DeSantis and his team have sought out corruption in government. He took action to suspend the Broward County sheriff who blatantly failed to prevent a mass shooting at a high school in Parkland,

THE SELF-SERVING PARTISAN CORRUPTION NEEDS TO BE ROOTED OUT IN ORDER TO RESTORE INTEGRITY TO OUR COUNTRY'S FOUNDATION.

Florida. The sheriff had multiple scandals in his department, including having received forty-five calls about the shooter prior to the incident, yet regretfully did not take action to protect the community.[70] DeSantis also asked the Florida Supreme Court to investigate failures in school security systems in the state. He has a track record of bringing justice and accountability.[71]

DeSantis improved integrity to Florida's election process. Florida had no trouble counting all their votes on election night of the 2020 presidential election, unlike several other suspicious states. After he was elected governor in 2018, DeSantis replaced the election supervisors in Broward and Palm Beach counties who had been notoriously negligent in their oversight of elections for decades. He also did not allow election policies to be changed due to Covid-19. Some states changed their laws and allowed more mail-in ballots, which increased fraud around the nation with ballot harvesting.[72]

As shown in Florida, DeSantis will search high and low for the leaven, the deeply rotted corruption festering in Washington, DC. He and his team will collect the rotten crumbs and will clean house. He will hold people accountable, prosecute criminal activity, model selfless sacrifice, and set the expectation of virtuous leadership. He has a track record of getting this done.

7

THE MESSENGER, JOHN THE BAPTIST

Look, I am sending my messenger ahead of you, and he will prepare your way. He is a voice shouting in the wilderness.

—MARK 1:2–3 NLT

Before cleaning house and rebuilding Washington, DC, a light needed to be shined on the political system to reveal the extensive corruption problem. In Jesus's day, John the Baptist was the man pointing out evil and preparing the way for a new system. He was an unusual man in appearance and habits, and no one expected him, not even his own parents since he was conceived in their old age (Luke 1:13-20). His clothing was camel hair, and he ate locusts and honey for food. From an early age, he lived in the wilderness on the western side of the Dead Sea (Matthew 3:1–4).

John the Baptist's mission in life was to prepare the way for the Messiah. In the Old Testament, when God had a message, He would bring a prophet to convey it.[73] Shortly before Jesus started His ministry, John the Baptist became the forerunner who declared that something new was coming. He was a messenger who shouted from the wilderness, preparing people's hearts for Jesus. As a truth-teller, he was not afraid to stir up controversy. He scornfully confronted hypocritical religious leaders. He even admonished King Herod, which led to his arrest and death (Matthew 14:3–12).

TRUMP'S JOB AS A MESSENGER IS COMPLETE, AND A NEW LEADERSHIP STYLE IS NEEDED IN THE NATION.

Like John the Baptist, Donald Trump is known as a unique character, particularly in the way he communicates. Trump has been a radical messenger who exposed lies and called for the swamp to be drained. In essence, Trump yelled to the political system, "Repent and change your ways. Justice is coming." He is a forerunner, and he is not afraid to bring a groundbreaking message that creates upheaval.

Many scholars believe that John the Baptist was the link between the Old and New Testaments. The Old Testament ends by referring to John the Baptist (the spirit of Elijah), and the New Testament begins with the birth and ministry of John the Baptist. He was the last of the Old Testament prophets. Like all Old Testament prophets, he was bringing something new, but was also preserving the old.[74]

John the Baptist was essentially a bridge; he had one foot in the Old Testament (the old way) and one foot in the New Testament (the new way).[75] Similarly, even though his message was radical, Trump's presidency showed that he had one foot in the establishment and one foot in the new political era. For example, during Covid-19, Trump delegated the responsibility of important decisions affecting the nation based on what career bureaucrat Anthony Fauci advised, resulting in disastrous decisions, fearmongering, and lockdowns in every state. Under Trump's leadership, instead of providing calm and reasonable recommendations, Fauci created panic and grossly faulty policies that adversely affected the nation.[76]

Since Trump was a bridge with one foot in the old era and one in the new, he was not as successful as he had hoped in draining the swamp of political corruption.

Like John the Baptist, Trump was an effective messenger and culture disrupter. He served his purpose and prepared the way for the one who will begin to remove corruption in Washington, DC. Trump's job as a messenger is complete, and a new leadership style is needed in the nation.

TRUMP PREPARED THE WAY FOR DESANTIS

Just as John the Baptist was pivotal in preparing for the Messiah, Trump has been crucial in readying the country for a DeSantis presidency. Trump has prepared the political climate, exposing establishment politicians as serving themselves more than their constituents. He brought a shift in the way Republicans viewed their own political party by creating a distinction between entrenched and reform-minded Republicans.

Trump was a catalyst for DeSantis winning the Republican primary for governor. When DeSantis ran for governor of Florida in 2018, his first task was to defeat agricultural commissioner Adam Putnam in the Republican primary.[77] Putnam was an establishment Republican and a "never Trumper."[78] In the past, Putnam may have won easily. Breaking the mold of traditional political party beliefs helped set the stage for DeSantis to defeat Putnam.

Trump endorsed DeSantis on Twitter boosting his support in the governor race. On June 22, 2018, Trump tweeted, "Ron is strong on Borders, tough on

Crime & big on Cutting Taxes - Loves our Military & our Vets. He will be a Great Governor & has my full Endorsement!"[79] Trump's support helped DeSantis win his governor race in 2018, positioning him in the right place at the right time. DeSantis's great success in leading during the pandemic, as well as his many accomplishments in Florida, launched him into the presidential run. Like John the Baptist preceding Jesus, Trump paved the way for a DeSantis presidency.

WATER SYMBOLICALLY PURIFIES

In the New Testament, one of the ways John the Baptist set the stage for Jesus's ministry was baptizing people in water. John's baptism symbolized a radical changing of one's ways to prepare for the Messiah.[80] Just as water cleans the outside of the body, water baptism represents an inward cleansing.

When John baptized the Israelites in the Jordan River, they were familiar with water being a metaphor for inward cleansing. In the Old Testament, Moses prepared Aaron and his sons for priesthood by washing them with water, symbolizing purification of sin (Leviticus 8:6). After being cleansed, the priests were allowed to perform sacrifices or prayers.[81] Still today, in the Catholic Mass before the Eucharist prayer, the priest will wash his hands while reciting Psalm 51:2, "Wash me, O Lord, from my iniquity and cleanse me from my sin."[82] The cleansing is not for dirt on the hands or body, but rather is a sign of inward purity.

Many Levitical laws given to the Jewish people were for cleaning the outside of one's body, aligning with sanitation methods in today's standards. Hand washing was specified before eating, upon waking, after using the toilet, and before prayer.[83] These were beneficial procedures in general for proper hygiene, but they also represented a deeper meaning.

In Jesus's day, ritual bathing in a "mikveh" (Hebrew for collection of water) became a standard practice for inward purification.[84] Jewish people were required to fully immerse themselves in the water before weddings, entering the Temple, or engaging in Jewish festivals. Even dishes and pots and pans would be considered kosher if dipped in a "mikveh."[85] Ceremonial cleaning was a metaphor for purging inner impurities.

OLD TESTAMENT WATER CROSSING BAPTISMS

In the Old Testament, crossing over or through water often was symbolic of water baptism, as the old was dying, bringing a new beginning.[86] When God decided to purge evil from the earth, He sent a flood. Only Noah and his family, who were in the ark, survived. The flood portrayed the old life passing away, being cleansed, and beginning a new life. 1 Peter 3 describes the flood as a parallel to baptism stating, "Only eight people were saved from drowning in that terrible flood. And that water is a picture of baptism, which now saves you, not by removing dirt from your body, but as a response to God from a clean conscience."[87] Noah being saved in the flood was not permanent, whereas those who are baptized in Jesus's name and profess Him as their Savior are saved forever.[88]

Another parallel to John's baptism is when Moses and the Israelites crossed the Red Sea, escaping slavery. In 1 Corinthians 10:2, the apostle Paul explains, "In the cloud and in the sea, all of them were baptized as followers of Moses."[89] When they left Egypt, the Israelites died to their old way of living and miraculously crossed the Red Sea on dry ground into a new beginning. It was a birth for the nation; the old was gone.[90] They had to develop a whole new life. Crossing the Red Sea was a symbol of baptism, leaving their leaven (impurities or sin) in Egypt. Similarly, when the Founding Fathers fled England and journeyed across the Atlantic Ocean, they resembled the Israelites crossing the Red Sea, being baptized into a new beginning.

Moses's baptism signified the Israelites were leaving their old life and were submitting to Moses as their leader. Despite God's miraculous provision of crossing the Red Sea on dry ground, under Moses's leadership the Israelites lacked self-control and disobeyed God. When Moses returned from Mt. Sinai, after meeting with God, he found them worshipping idols.[91] They had returned to their old ways of living.

Forty years later, when the Israelites were preparing

to enter the Promised Land, they experienced another figurative baptism. God stopped the Jordan River from flowing and Joshua led them across into the Promised Land.[92] Crossing the Jordan River meant the Israelites were once again leaving behind the old (the wilderness) and entering into a new life in the new land.

Being baptized under Joshua's leadership resulted in a different outcome than Moses's baptism. In the Promised Land, under Joshua's leadership, the Israelites were able to conquer their enemies.[93] They were faithful to God and did not revert to worshipping idols.[94] Joshua is often seen as a foreshadowing of Jesus because he was able to defeat darkness and was a faithful servant of God.[95] Illustrating a significant parallel, Joshua's baptism of the Jewish people happened in the same place Jesus was baptized, in the Jordan River.[96] Jesus was baptized at the beginning of his ministry before conquering the Enemy. Similarly, Joshua's water crossing baptism occurred prior to defeating giants in the Promised Land. Joshua's success symbolized the power of new life when baptized in Jesus's name.

Just as Moses's baptism was not as effective as Joshua's, Trump's attempt to defeat the enemy and purify the government was not successful. Trump led us out of political enslavement, setting the stage for the political messiah to reclaim the Promised Land. Likewise, John's baptisms paved the way for when Jesus's sacrifice would provide life changing power to cleanse sins.[97]The real transformation illustrated in baptism was not possible in John's baptisms or in the Old Testament baptisms, because Jesus had not yet conquered sin and death by dying on the cross.[98]

As a John the Baptist figure, Trump did not have the power to bring real transformation to the government. The true change will come with his successor. Trump paved the way and radically changed the political atmosphere, preparing for an inward cleaning in the heart of government. The political messiah and his team will metaphorically "baptize" the government, purifying and bringing lasting change.

8

THE POLITICAL MESSIAH

See, I am doing a new thing! Now it springs up; do you not perceive it?

—ISAIAH 43:19A NIV

Jesus brought the power of new life and demonstrated how to be a successful leader. The world often assumes the most successful leaders are ruthless, self-serving, and egotistical. Jesus exhibited a new standard of operating as a leader. Before He came to earth, people were expecting the Messiah to look like a royal king and did not expect someone who blended in, unrecognized.[99] Isaiah prophesied saying, "He had no stately form or

The world often assumes the most successful leaders are ruthless, self-serving, and egotistical.

55

majestic splendor that we would look at Him, nor appearance that we would be attracted to Him" (Isaiah 53:2 AMP). Many did not believe and recognize Jesus because He did not resemble what they presumed of the Messiah. His focus was on his mission, rather than His appearance or reputation.

SERVANT OF ALL

The primary leadership quality used to describe Jesus is that of a servant leader. In the book of Isaiah, which contains dozens of prophecies of Jesus's life, Jesus is referred to as the Servant.[100] Isaiah 42:1 prophesies of Jesus, saying, "Behold, my servant, whom I uphold; my chosen, in whom my soul delighteth: I have put my Spirit upon him; he will bring forth justice to the Gentiles" (ASV). As a servant leader, Jesus submitted completely to God the Father, saying, "For I have come down from heaven not to do my will but to do the will of him who sent me" (John 6:38 NIV). He was a humble servant on a mission to conquer the Enemy and take away the curse of sin. Jesus's mission was destined by God, and He carried it out fully. When He returns, as prophesied in the book of Revelation, He will come as a warrior bringing justice and a new heaven and earth.

Two of the most prominent features of Jesus's life were humility and sacrifice. He said, "Those who exalt themselves will be humbled, and those who humble themselves will be exalted" (Luke 14:11 NIV). Referring to Himself, Jesus also said, "The Son of Man did not come to be served, but to serve" (Matthew 20:28 NIV). At the Last Supper before Jesus's death, His disciples were stunned when He washed their feet. The task of washing another's feet was usually reserved for the lowest members of society. This was a paradigm shift. Jesus taught, "Whoever wants to be a leader among you must be your servant" (Matthew 20:26 NLT).

In 2022, retired navy captain Dan Bean described DeSantis's main attribute as a "servant leader." Bean expounded, "As someone who has served side by side with him, he is selfless. He will do what is in your best interest. . . . He is a true servant leader."[101] In an interview with Piers Morgan, DeSantis described himself as "a vessel for the aspirations of the people I represent."[102] Like our Founding Fathers, DeSantis is a selfless leader, putting the needs of his people above his own self-interest. In humility he says, "All I'm interested in doing is getting things done and accomplishing things. I don't need a title. I don't need fanfare."[103] Like Jesus, DeSantis is a true leader who will humbly serve our country.

CLEANING A CORRUPT SYSTEM

During His earthly ministry, Jesus had a mission to clean out corruption in the religious system. He frequently challenged hypocrites, particularly the religious leaders of His day. They had the illusion of being righteous, but their behavior showed differently. Jesus confronted the

Pharisees, saying, "You are so careful to clean the outside of the cup and the dish, but inside you are filthy—full of greed and self-indulgence!" (Matthew 23:25 NLT). They elevated themselves and their reputation rather than serving others. When leaders lack integrity and manipulate others to benefit themselves, the leaven easily diffuses into the rest of the community. This is why Jesus had scathing criticism for puffed-up leaders who cared more about their own comfort and how they looked rather than doing the right thing.

Another example of Jesus cleansing corruption is when He cleared out the temple (John 2). It was just before Passover, and the Israelites were preparing their homes for the Feast of Unleavened Bread, thoroughly cleaning and checking to ensure that they did not possess any leaven. It was a time to purge out any impurities or pride. Jesus used the occasion to clean His Father's house of self-interest in the religious system (John 2:16).

Jesus went to the temple, and He found dishonest people who were selling doves, oxen, and sheep, along with the money changers who were exchanging currency. He made a whip and drove them all out, saying, "Get these things out of here. Stop turning my Father's house into a marketplace!" (John 2:16 NLT). The religious hypocrites were profiteering, contaminating God's holy place of worship and prayer; it was time to clean house.

The temple was run by elite aristocrats, including Annas, a high priest, and his sons and sons-in-law, who were assistant priests. The sons of Annas determined which animal sacrifices would be considered acceptable, and they charged an inspection fee. Intentionally, they determined that the animal was unacceptable, and therefore the person would need to buy one of their own animals, which was sold at a premium price.[104] Jesus forced dishonest hypocrites out of the temple. He gained strong approval from those who were being manipulated, as well as vehement opposition from the religious leaders He confronted.

STANDING UP TO EVIL

In Florida, Governor DeSantis has stood up to injustice "with military precision," as Focus on the Family's Jim Daly alluded to in an interview with DeSantis in 2022.[105] He has accomplished more in his state by standing against evil than any other political leader has done anywhere in the nation. Some of the legislation he helped pass in his state protects free speech on social media for political candidates, protects people from "woke" religion by rejecting books with ideological indoctrination, prohibits puberty blockers and sex change operations on minors, bans digital currency,[106] protects women athletes from transgender participation,[107] and ensures that people must use public bathrooms according to one's gender assigned at birth.[108]

DeSantis leads with a holy determination to protect his people. He is not afraid to confront evil. He signed the heartbeat bill, which is the strongest pro-life law in Florida's modern history.[109] He describes one of his qualities as "being willing to stand in the fire when it gets really really hot and not back down under pressure."[110] In 2022, Jim Daly told DeSantis, "Thank you for being such a great example of how to do this well. You have admirers beyond Florida; the whole nation is watching you."[111]

Jesus is the best example of one who acted based upon conviction rather than a desire for popularity. Repeatedly, Jesus explained why He was driven to act in such a way. He said that He only did what God guided Him to do. Jesus demonstrates when acting out of divine conviction, you rise to a level that is immune to people's approval; only then can your actions turn the tide of an entire culture. During the pandemic, DeSantis gained support not only in his own state and in other states, but he was also recognized at an international level. His courageous leadership was a glimmer of hope around the globe during a dark time.[112] In reality, DeSantis operated as a presidential leader far more effectively than President Trump did during that time.

DeSantis has continued to shine as an unprecedented leader in protecting his state from woke ideology, especially in regard to children. The woke movement has crossed a line that will in turn cause forfeiting of the ground they have taken. Attempting to persuade and defile even the youngest school-aged children will cost them in the 2024 election. If adults decide to try to change their gender, they have the freedom to do so, but intentionally targeting children with propaganda takes it too far. Parents rose up during the pandemic, standing against mask mandates and school closures. Online learning has allowed parents to become more aware of what their children are being taught in school. There is a rising anti-woke majority, particularly among parents of young children. DeSantis has demonstrated that he will fiercely stand up for his people, and now more than ever, his leadership is needed as president of the United States.

LAYING DOWN YOUR REPUTATION

There are paradoxical truths in the Bible that are in stark contrast to the world's paradigm. The people of the world pursue fame, power, and money. Jesus said, "Whoever loses his life for My sake will find it" (Matthew 16:25). "Whoever desires to become great among you, let him be your servant" (Matthew 20:26). "He who humbles himself will be exalted" (Matthew 23:12). You find true purpose in surrendering your reputation to God and seeking His plan for your life, and this purpose and fulfillment is far greater than what can be imagined. Jesus sacrificed His own comfort and prestige in order to follow God's plan for His life. Referring to Jesus, Paul said, "He humbled Himself and became obedient to the point of death, even the death of the cross. Therefore God also has highly exalted Him and given Him the name which is above every name" (Philippians 2:8–9). Jesus's life reveals the paradox that great leadership begins with humility.

People with puffed-up hearts are incapable of being sacrificial leaders. Their own agendas and reputations are their idols. With God as the foundation, humility comes more naturally. We do not see ourselves as grandiose when we have a true relationship with God. We are submitting to a higher authority. The focus is on how we can serve others, not on who can serve us.

Jesus paid the ultimate sacrifice. He willingly gave up His reputation and His life for those who believe in Him. It is not a natural desire to lay down your reputation for the sake of others. When a leader acts in such a noble way, it has a spiritual impact on all those around them. Jesus said it best: "There is no greater love than to lay down one's life for one's friends" (John 15:13 NLT). We need more politicians who are willing to sacrifice their reputations

> DESANTIS IS A RARE LEADER WHO VALUES SACRIFICE AND SERVING HIS COUNTRY OVER HIS OWN COMFORT, FINANCIAL GAIN, AND PRESTIGE.

and well-being to do the right thing, no matter the cost.

Our country was founded on self-sacrifice and bravery. The Founding Fathers risked their lives and fortunes for our freedom. When the fifty-six men signed the Declaration of Independence, they risked it all for freedom: nine signers sacrificed their lives in the war, twelve fought in battles, five became prisoners of war, seventeen lost their property, and five went into debt funding the war.[113] They believed in the cause of freedom and committed their lives to create the nation. Throughout our nation's history, honorable patriots have humbly served our country for the cause of freedom.

DeSantis is a rare leader who values sacrifice and serving his country over his own comfort, financial gain, and prestige. Ron DeSantis graduated from Yale University with a bachelor's degree and from Harvard University with a law degree. Normally someone in his position would pursue a six-figure income and a prestigious job. Instead, DeSantis, willing to lay down his life and career for others, enrolled in the navy during wartime. After serving in the navy for fifteen years, he ran for the United States Congress and was elected to represent Florida's 6th district in the US House of Representatives.[114] Ron DeSantis is a patriot who embodies the type of self-sacrifice that our Founding Fathers demonstrated for our country.

In 2018, Ron DeSantis was elected as governor of the state of Florida. During Covid-19, Governor DeSantis laid down his reputation and had the courage to follow his conviction and wise counsel, going against the establishment. In turn, Florida was able to enjoy freedom like no other state in our nation. People from our country and around the world sent notes of gratitude to his office and many others thanked him in person for his brave leadership during the pandemic.[115] We need a valiant leader who will lay down his reputation for the sake of our nation. Governor DeSantis is a political messiah.

THE ANOINTED ONE

The word "messiah" comes from the Hebrew word *mashiach*, meaning "the anointed one" or "the chosen one."[116] The anointing represents the Spirit of God. Jesus had an anointing to empower His ministry. He began His earthly ministry by saying, "The Spirit of the Sovereign LORD is upon me, for the LORD has anointed me to bring good news to the poor" (Isaiah 61:1; Luke 4:18 NLT). Other Israelite kings, priests, and prophets also were anointed with God's Spirit. The anointing empowers people to do specifically what God has called them to do.[117]

In 1 Samuel 16, the Lord told the prophet Samuel to fill his horn with oil and to find and anoint the new king whom God had chosen. Samuel went to search for the new king at the house of Jesse the Bethlehemite. Jesse had eight sons. He quickly brought out his eldest son, assuming he would be the one who would be anointed, and presented him to Samuel. However, he was not the chosen one. Jesse continued to present one son after another to Samuel, but none of them were the right one. Samuel asked Jesse if he had any other sons. Jesse called for his youngest son, David, who was in the shepherd's field. When Samuel saw David, he declared that he was going to be the new king and the one whom he would anoint. Then Samuel poured the oil on David's head, "and the Spirit of the LORD came powerfully upon David from that day on" (1 Samuel 16:13 NLT).

A few chapters later, we see that David's anointing empowered him to fight the giant, Goliath, and win. In our own strength, we have limited ability to accomplish God's work, but with the Spirit of God, we can do the impossible. "'Not by might nor by power, but by My Spirit,' says the LORD of hosts" (Zechariah 4:6). With God's help, Ron DeSantis will be empowered to lead a team that will conquer political giants and clean out corruption. I believe he is chosen and equipped by God for this specific mission.

9

RECLAIMING THE PROMISED LAND

This is my command-- be strong and courageous! Do not be afraid or discouraged. For the Lord your God is with you wherever you go.

—JOSHUA 1:9 NLT

When Joshua and the Israelites were heading into the Promised Land to fight their first battle, the battle against Jericho, some scholars believe Jesus appeared to him.[118] Joshua looked up and a man was standing in front of him with his sword drawn. The man said, "I am the commander of the LORD's army. . . . Take off your sandals, for the place where you are standing is holy" (Joshua 5:13–15 NLT). The man, thought by many to have been Jesus, reassured Joshua that God had given the Israelites victory over the people of Jericho, whom they were getting ready to fight. After the supernatural encounter, Joshua and the Israelites went forth in confidence, knowing that the Lord was on their side and that the battle had already been won. As we charge ahead to conquer political giants, God is fighting for justice and righteousness in our nation. We do not battle alone, but we have the Lord on our side.

Joshua leading his people into the Promised Land is a parallel to the Messiah, Jesus. Joshua and Jesus have the same name in Hebrew—Yehoshua—which means salvation.[119] The warrior Joshua is a foreshadowing of Jesus, who is the commander of the Lord's army. Just as Joshua courageously entered into the Promised Land knowing that God was with them, we can have the same confidence in God as we move into this next political season.

WHAT IS OUR PROMISED LAND?

Imagine our country being led by God-fearing, self-sacrificing leaders we can trust. Imagine politicians and government officials being held to the same standard as the citizens of this country. Imagine our institutions being cleaned of corruption and waste.

OVERCOMING GIANTS

In order to possess our political Promised Land, we must overcome giants. Some of the giants are the usual targets—biased media, anti-God agenda, special interests, and woke religion. The key to entering the Promised Land, though, is not to be solely focused on those enemies. There is a bigger, more powerful giant than the usual ones people refer to: our unbelief. The apostle Paul explains why a generation of Israelites did not go into the Promised Land: "They were not able to enter, because of their unbelief" (Hebrews 3:19 NIV). Like the Israelites, we have become hopeless for change and have stopped believing that integrity can be restored to our government. When we let darkness tie our hands with unbelief and forget that God is more than able to move and work in our country, we block our entrance into the Promised Land. The more we watch the negative news

WHEN EVERYONE ELSE SEES DOOM AND DESTRUCTION, WE SEE HOW GOD WILL EMPOWER US TO BRING INTEGRITY BACK TO OUR POLITICAL SYSTEM.

and stir up hatred in our hearts, the more our unbelief becomes like kryptonite to God's mighty power.

We have a choice to make in our country. Do we continue to wander in the desert, frustrated and hopeless, thinking that political corruption is a giant too big for us to overcome—or do we elevate God, His great love for this country, and His ability to move mountains?

Let us choose to be like Joshua and Caleb. When everyone else sees doom and destruction, we see how God will empower us to bring integrity back to our political system. We see that we are able to bring justice to government systems. "Now all glory to God, who is able, through his mighty power at work within us, to accomplish infinitely more than we might ask or think" (Ephesians 3:20 NLT). God wants to clean house of the politically corrupt and raise up self-sacrificing, courageous leaders in our country.

OPPORTUNITY IS KNOCKING

God uses different leaders for different purposes. Where we were in 2016 is a very different place than where we are now. As a nation, our eyes have been opened to the broken political system—thanks to Donald Trump and his unique ability to disrupt the status quo. Trump's message of draining the swamp, along with the government's quest for control that was exposed during the pandemic, has resulted in a nation ripe for reform. The next step is bringing in a servant leader with a track record of reform to clean out Washington, DC, and begin to restore integrity to our government.

America, God's divine Providence is still at work within our nation, just as it has been throughout our history. The Founding Fathers showed us that the Lord is with us and that He has a good plan for our country. Just as God's hand gave the Israelites a messenger leader for the exodus from Egypt and a warrior leader for entering into the Promised Land, God is preparing and directing the leader our country needs for this time period. The leader and his team will clean out political leaven and will also search his own heart for impurities. The leader for this season had a forerunner who paved the way for the work that will be done during his presidency.

Transformation is possible in our country. Realizing the unique season we are in, we need to seize the opportunity at hand and begin to restore our country's integrity.

Ron DeSantis is the political messiah, like Joshua, who will clean house and lead us in reclaiming the Promised Land. He is a courageous warrior empowered to strategically fight and defeat darkness in Washington, DC. Following Jesus's example, DeSantis is a self-sacrificing leader willing to lay down his reputation and do what is right.

In this nation at this moment in time, we have a window of opportunity. People are unsatisfied with the old way and long for change in our political system now more than ever. The leader empowered by God in this season to take the land is—Ron DeSantis.

ENDNOTES

1   Michael Ruszala, "Two Nations Under God: Israel and America's Foundation," Ascension, https://media.ascensionpress.com/2019/07/04/two-nations-god/.

2   Angela Kamrath, *The Miracle of America*, 3rd ed. (Houston: American Heritage Education Foundation, 2020), 54.

3   Douglas S. Winnail, "Miracles of the American Revolution," Tomorrow's World, July-August 2017, https://www.tomorrowsworld.org/magazines/2017/july-august/miracles-of-the-american-revolution.

4   Michael Medved, *The American Miracle: Divine Providence in the Rise of the Republic* (New York: Forum Books, 2016), 32.

5   Medved, *American Miracle*, 365.

6   "Mayflower and Mayflower Compact," Plimouth Patuxet Musuems, https://plimoth.org/for-students/homework-help/mayflower-and-mayflower-compact.

7   Kamrath, *Miracle*, 54.

8   Kamrath, *Miracle*, 67–68.

9   John Winthrop, "A Model of Christian Charity," in *A Library of American Literature, Vol. 1, Early Colonial Literature, 1607–1675*, ed. Edmund Clarence Stedman and Ellen Mackay Hutchinson (New York: Charles L. Webster & Company, 1888), 304–307.

10 Kamrath, *Miracle,* 67.

11 Kamrath, *Miracle,* 129, 140.

12 Kamrath, *Miracle,* 236.

13 Kamrath, *Miracle,* 129, 140.

14 Kamrath, *Miracle,* 161–162, 278.

ENDNOTES

15 Stephen Flick, "Thomas Paine Argues 'No King But God,'" January 8, 2023, Christian Heritage Fellowship, https://christianheritagefellowship.com/thomas-paine-argues-no-king-but-god/.

16 "Revolutionary War," History.com, https://www.history.com/topics/american-revolution/american-revolution-history.

17 Kamrath, *Miracle,* 224–225.

18 John Witherspoon, "The Dominion of Providence over the Passions of Men," in *Political Sermons of the American Founding Era: 1730–1805,* ed, Ellis Sandoz (Indianapolis: Liberty Fund, 1990), 533.

19 "Declaration of Independence: A Transcription." *National Archives,* 4 Jul. 1776, www.archives.gov.

20 Kamrath, *Miracle,* 224.

21 Susie Federer and William Federer, *Miracles in American History* (Virginia Beach: Amerisearch, Inc, 2012), 17–19.

22 "Articles of Confederation (1777)." National Archives, 4 Jul. 1776, www.archives.gov.

23 Matthew Spalding, "The Formation of the Constitution," September 14, 2007, The Heritage Foundation, https://www.heritage.org.

24 Medved, *American* Miracle, 120.

25 Medved, *American Miracle,* 121.

26 "History of 'In God We Trust,'" In God We Trust, https://ingodwetrust.com/about/history-of-in-god-we-trust/.

27 "History of 'In God We Trust.'"

28 "H.R.619 - An Act to Provide That All United States Currency Shall Bear the Inscription 'In God We Trust.'" *Congress.Gov,* 11 Jul. 1955, www.congress.gov.

29 Kamrath, *Miracle* p. preface.

30 Kamrath, *Miracle* p. preface.

31 Stephen McDowell, "The Forefathers Monument: A Matrix of Liberty," Providence Foundation, https://providencefoundation.com.

32 Dave Pelland, *Faith and Freedom: The National Monument to the Forefathers* (Monument Publishing, 2015), 12.

33 Norman S. Ream, "Morality in America," July 1, 1993, Foundation for Economic Education, https://fee.org/articles/morality-in-america/.

34 "The Pilgrims' Formula to Save America," from *Monumental: In Search of America's National Treasure* video, directed by Duane Barnhart (Word Films P & D, 2012).

35 Medved, *American Miracle,* 360.

ENDNOTES

36 T. Harv Eker, Good Reads. https://www.goodreads.com/quotes/977259-it-s-not-enough-to-be-in-right-place-at-right.

37 "Drain the Swamp," Wikipedia, accessed June 1, 2023, en.wikipedia.org/wiki/Drain_the_swamp.

38 "Drain the Swamp," Wikipedia.

39 Alan Draper, "The Top 17 Hillary Clinton Scandals," December 12, 2022, Business2Community, https://www.business2community.com/government-politics/the-top-17-hillary-clinton-scandals-01337217.

40 Ron DeSantis, *The Courage to Be Free* p.158-169 (New York: Broadside Books, 2023).

41 DeSantis, *Courage,* 158-169.

42 DeSantis, *Courage.*

43 Rabbi YY Jacobson, "Why Did Moses Not Enter the Holy Land?" May 27, 2018, YouTube video, 59:22, youtube.com/watch?v=KgttzxoEzaM&list=PPSV.

44 Rabbi Mordechai Torczyner, "Yehoshua—The Book of Joshua—From Slaves to Israelis," December 26, 2017, YouTube video, 27:33, https://www.youtube.com/watch?v=vjlKZJQ4kJo.

45 Jacobson, "Why Did Moses Not Enter the Holy Land?"

46 Jacobson, "Why Did Moses Not Enter the Holy Land?"

47 Jacobson, "Why Did Moses Not Enter the Holy Land?"

48 "How Old Was Joshua When He Entered the Promised Land?" Never Thirsty, https://www.neverthirsty.org/bible-qa/qa-archives/question/how-old-was-joshua-when-he-entered-the-promise-land/.

49 Torczyner, "Yehoshua."

50 Torczyner, "Yehoshua."

51 DeSantis, *Courage,* 129-145.

52 Patrick Lencioni. Good Reads, https://www.goodreads.com/quotes/218850-remember-teamwork-begins-by-building-trust-and-the-only-waywww.goodreads.com.

53 Kurt Bardella, "Trump didn't drain the swamp. Now Biden may drown him in it," May 21, 2020, USA Today, https://www.usatoday.com/story/opinion/2020/05/21/trump-didnt-drain-swamp-biden-drown-him-column/5228137002/.

54 Kathryn Dunn Tenpas. "And Then There Were Ten: With 85% Turnover across President Trump'S A Team, Who Remains?" *Brookings,* 13 Apr. 2020, www.brookings.edu.

ENDNOTES

55   John Maxwell, "Three Components of Cultivating Culture," December 1, 2021, 37:40, *The John Maxwell Leadership Podcast*, https://johnmaxwellleadershippodcast.com/episodes/john-maxwell-three-components-of-cultivating-culture.

56   Maxwell, "Three Components."

57   "12 Behaviors Leaders Model to Develop a Leadership Culture," March 2, 2021, The John Maxwell Co., corporatesolutions.johnmaxwell.com/blog/behaviors-leaders-model-to-develop-a-leadership-culture/.

58   DeSantis, *Courage,* 92.

59   Piers Morgan, "Piers Morgan vs. Ron DeSantis," March 23, 2023, YouTube video, 1:05:16, youtube.com/watch?v=vIj4LUPlgKc&t=10s.

60   "Public Trust in Government: 1958–2022," June 6, 2022, Pew Research Center, https://www.pewresearch.org/politics/2022/06/06/public-trust-in-government-1958-2022/.

61   Albert Einstein, Good Reads, https://www.goodreads.com/quotes/29875-the-world-is-a-dangerous-place-to-live-not-because.

62   Rabbi Alon Anava, "Pesach—The real meaning behind cleaning your 'Chametz,'" March 16, 2018, YouTube video, 1:57:03, youtube.com/watch?v=cyG4OrdmQ6U.

63   "Preparing for Passover," Hebrew for Christians, https://www.hebrew4christians.com/Holidays/Spring_Holidays/Pesach/Preparations/preparations.html#loaded.

64   Rabbi Alan Green, "What is Chametz? (It's not Just Yeast)," March 16, 2018, YouTube video, 5:29, youtube.com/watch?v=HY2cJKEH4D4.

65   Green, "What is Chametz?"

66   "The Root Cause of All Sin," Messiah-Of-God, www.messiah-of-god.com/root-cause-of-all-sin.html.

67   James Bovard, "If the Government Lies to You," April 6, 2018, James Bovard, https://jimbovard.com/blog/2018/04/06/if-the-government-lies-to-you/.

68   DeSantis, *Courage.*

69   DeSantis, *Courage.*

70   DeSantis, *Courage*, 116-118.

71   DeSantis, *Courage*, 116-118.

72   DeSantis, *Courage,* 134-138.

73   John Ritenbaugh. "Prophets and Prophecy (Part 2)." Church of the Great God, www.cgg.org.

74   John Ritenbaugh, "Prophets and Prophecy," Bible Tools, www.Bibletools.org.

ENDNOTES

75   "John the Baptist is the Prophet Who Links the Old Testament to the New Testament," Christian Prophecy, http://www.christianprophecy.org.uk/otnt/ot07John.html.

76   DeSantis, *Courage,* 158.

77   DeSantis, *Courage,* 75-81.

78   DeSantis, *Courage,* 76.

79   DeSantis, *Courage,* 78.

80   (2015). *Matthew 3:11 NLT.* YouVersion. www.bible.com

81   (2015). *Exodus 30:18-20 NLT.* YouVersion. www.bible.com

82   Philip Kosloski. "Why Do Priests Wash Their Hands During Mass?" Aleteia, 10 Jul. 2021, aleteia.org.

83   (2015). *Leviticus 15:1-16:28 NLT.* YouVersion. www.bible.com

84   "Ancient Jews and Cleanliness." Early Church History, earlychurchhistory.org.

85   "Tevilah: Immersion of Vessels." Chabad.Org, www.chabad.org.

86   James Williams. "Old Testament Background for Christian Baptism." Seed and Water for Souls, www.seedandwater.org.

87   (2015). *1 Peter 3:20b-21a NLT.* YouVersion. www.bible.com

88   (2015). *Mark 16:16 NLT.* YouVersion. www.bible.com

89   (2015). *1 Corinthians 10:2 NLT.* YouVersion. www.bible.com

90   Alastair Roberts. "Rightly Dividing Red Sea."*Rightly Dividing the Red Sea,* 3 Mar. 2020, www.thegospelcoalition.org.

91   (2015). *Exodus 32:19 NLT.* YouVersion. www.bible.com

92   (2015). *Joshua 4:23 NLT.* YouVersion. www.bible.com

93   (2015). *Joshua 6:1-27 NLT.* YouVersion. www.bible.com

94   (2015). *Joshua 24:1-28 NLT.* YouVersion. www.bible.com

95   John Oakes. "Old Testament Background for Christian Baptism." A Study of Foreshadows in the Book of Joshua, 29 Aug. 2018, evidenceforchristianity.org.

96   (2015). *Matthew 3:13-16 NLT.* YouVersion. www.bible.com

97   (2015). *Acts 19:4-5 NLT.* YouVersion. www.bible.com

98   (2015). *1Corinthians 15:55-57 NLT.* YouVersion. www.bible.com

99   Joseph Tkach. "Jesus Christ: The Unexpected Messiah." Grace Communion International, www.gci.org.

100 Sandra L. Richter, "Epic of Eden: Isaiah," September 1, 2019, Seedbed, https://my.seedbed.com/product/the-epic-of-eden-isaiah/.

101 Ron DeSantis. "Honor, Courage, Commitment," September 23, 2022, YouTube video, :30, youtube.com/watch?v=wz_8tnqWS2M.

102 Piers Morgan, "Piers Morgan vs. Ron DeSantis."

103   Piers Morgan, "Piers Morgan vs. Ron DeSantis."

104   Jay Mack, "Jesus' First Cleaning of the Temple at the Passover," The Teaching Ministry of Jay Mack, https://jaymack.net/bs-jesus-first-cleansing-of-the-temple-at-the-passover-john-2-13-22/.

105   "Being a Positive Force for the Family," June 23, 2023, *Focus on the Family Broadcast*, https://www.focusonthefamily.com/episodes/broadcast/being-a-positive-force-for-the-family/.

106   "SB 7054: Central Bank Digital Currency," The Florida Senate, https://www.flsenate.gov/Session/Bill/2023/7054.

107   DeSantis, *Courage,* 131-132.

108   "CS/HB 1521—Facility Requirements Based on Sex," Florida House of Representatives, https://www.myfloridahouse.gov/Sections/Bills/billsdetail.aspx?BillId=78388.

109   DeSantis, *Courage*, 118–145.

110   Piers Morgan, "Piers Morgan vs. Ron DeSantis."

111   "Being a Positive Force for the Family," *Focus on the Family Broadcast*.

112   DeSantis, *Courage* xii.

113   "Do You Know Many Founding Fathers Died or Lost Their Fortunes for Freedom?" Patriot Academy, https://www.patriotacademy.com/dyk-087/.

114   DeSantis, *Courage,* 34-44.

115   DeSantis, *Courage* xii.

116   Bible Hub, s.v. mashiach, 4899, biblehub.com/hebrew/4899.htm.

117   Jonathan Cahn, "The Anointed," May 21, 2021, Hope of the World, hopeoftheworld.org.

118   "Commander of the Lord's Army," November 29, 2010, Ligonier Ministries, ligonier.org/learn/devotionals/commander-lords-army.

119   "Jesus, Jeshua, Joshua, Yeshua, Yehoshua." *First Fruits of Zion*, torahportions.ffoz.org.

BIBLIOGRAPHY

Anava, Rabbi Alon. "*Pesach—The real meaning behind cleaning your 'Chametz.'*" *March 16, 2018. YouTube video. 1:57:03.* youtube.com/watch?v=cyG4OrdmQ6U.

"Ancient Jews and Cleanliness." *Early Church History,* earlychurchhistory.org.

"Articles of Confederation (1777)." *National Archives,* 4 Jul. 1776, www.archives. gov.

Bardella, Kurt. "*Trump didn't drain the swamp. Now Biden may drown him in it.*" May 21, 2020, USA Today. https://www.usatoday.com/story/opinion/2020/05/21/trump-didnt-drain-swamp-biden-drown-him-column/5228137002/.

"Being a Positive Force for the Family," June 23, 2023, *Focus on the Family Broadcast,* https://www.focusonthefamily.com/episodes/broadcast/being-a-positive-force-for-the-family/.

Bible Hub. S.V. Mashiach, 4899. biblehub.com/hebrew/4899.htm.

Bovard, James. "If the Government Lies to You." April 6, 2018. https://jimbovard.com/blog/2018/04/06/if-the-government-lies-to-you/.

Cahn, Jonathan. "*The Anointed.*" May 21, 2021, Hope of the World. hopeoftheworld.org.

"*Commander of the Lord's Army.*" November 29, 2010, Ligonier Ministries. ligonier.org/learn/devotionals/commander-lords-army.

"*CS/HB 1521—Facility Requirements Based on Sex.*" Florida House of Representatives. https://www.myfloridahouse.gov/Sections/Bills/billsdetail. aspx?BillId=78388.

BIBLIOGRAPHY

"Declaration of Independence: A Transcription." *National Archives*, 4 Jul. 1776. www.archives.gov.

DeSantis, Ron. *"Honor, Courage, Commitment."* September 23, 2022. YouTube video. youtube.com/watch?v=wz_8tnqWS2M.

DeSantis, Ron. *The Courage to Be Free*. New York: Broadside Books, 2023.

"Do You Know Many Founding Fathers Died or Lost Their Fortunes for Freedom?" Patriot Academy. https://www.patriotacademy.com/dyk-087/.

"Drain the Swamp," Wikipedia, accessed June 1, 2023, en.wikipedia.org/wiki/Drain_the_swamp.

Alan Draper, "The *Top 17 Hillary Clinton Scandals,*" December 12, 2022, Business2Community, https://waww.business2community.com/government-politics/the-top-17-hillary-clinton-scandals-01337217.

Dunn Tenpas, Kathryn. "And Then There Were Ten: With 85% Turnover across President Trump'S A Team, Who Remains?" *Brookings*, 13 Apr. 2020. www.brookings.edu.

Einstein, Albert. Good Reads. https://www.goodreads.com/quotes/29875-the-world-is-a-dangerous-place-to-live-not-because.

Eker, T. Harv. Good Reads. https://www.goodreads.com/quotes/977259-it-s-not-enough-to-be-in-right-place-at-right.

Federer, Susie and William Federer. *Miracles in American History*. Virginia Beach: Amerisearch, Inc, 2012.

Flick, Stephen. *"Thomas Paine Argues 'No King But God.'"* January 8, 2023, Christian Heritage Fellowship. https://christianheritagefellowship.com/thomas-paine-argues-no-king-but-god/.

Green, Rabbi Alan. *"What is Chametz? (It's not Just Yeast)." March 16, 2018, YouTube video. 5:29.* youtube.com/watch?v=HY2cJKEH4D4.

"History of 'In God We Trust,'" In God We Trust, https://ingodwetrust.com/about/history-of-in-god-we-trust/.

"How Old Was Joshua When He Entered the Promised Land?" Never Thirsty, https://www.neverthirsty.org/bible-qa/qa-archives/question/how-old-was-joshua-when-he-entered-the-promise-land/.

"H.R.619 - An Act to Provide That All United States Currency Shall Bear the Inscription 'In God We Trust.'" *Congress.Gov*, 11 Jul. 1955, www.congress.gov.

BIBLIOGRAPHY

Jacobson, Rabbi YY. "*Why Did Moses Not Enter the Holy Land?*" May 27, 2018, YouTube video, 59:22, youtube.com/watch?v=KgttzxoEzaM&list=PPSV.

"Jesus, Jeshua, Joshua, Yeshua, Yehoshua." *First Fruits of Zion*, torahportions.ffoz.org.

"*John the Baptist is the Prophet Who Links the Old Testament to the New Testament*." Christian Prophecy. http://www.christianprophecy.org.uk/otnt/ot07John.html.

Kamrath, Angela. *The Miracle of America*, 3rd ed. Houston: American Heritage Education Foundation, 2020.

Kosloski, Philip. "Why Do Priests Wash Their Hands During Mass?" *Aleteia*, 10 Jul. 2021, aleteia.org.

Lencioni, Patrick. Good Reads. https://www.goodreads.com/quotes.

Mack, Jay. "*Jesus' First Cleaning of the Temple at the Passover*." The Teaching Ministry of Jay Mack. https://jaymack.net/bs-jesus-first-cleansing-of-the-temple-at-the-passover-john-2-13-22/.

Maxwell, John. "*12 Behaviors Leaders Model to Develop a Leadership Culture.*" March 2, 2021. The John Maxwell Co. corporatesolutions.johnmaxwell.com/blog/behaviors-leaders-model-to-develop-a-leadership-culture/.

Maxwell, John. "*Three Components of Cultivating Culture.*" December 1, 2021. *37:40. The John Maxwell Leadership Podcast. https://johnmaxwellleadershippodcast.com/episodes/john-maxwell-three-components-of-cultivating-culture.*

"*Mayflower and Mayflower Compact.*" Plimouth Patuxet Musuems, https://plimoth.org/for-students/homework-help/mayflower-and-mayflower-compact.

McDowell, Stephen. "*The Forefathers Monument: A Matrix of Liberty.*" Providence Foundation. https://providencefoundation.com.

Medved, Michael. *The American Miracle: Divine Providence in the Rise of the Republic.* New York: Forum Books, 2016.

Morgan, Piers. "*Piers Morgan vs. Ron DeSantis.*" March 23, 2023. YouTube video. 1:05:16. youtube.com/watch?v=vIj4LUPlgKc&t=10s.

Oakes, John. "Old Testament Background for Christian Baptism." *A Study of Foreshadows in the Book of Joshua*. 29 Aug. 2018. evidenceforchristianity.org.

Pelland, Dave. *Faith and Freedom: The National Monument to the Forefathers.* Monument Publishing, 2015.

BIBLIOGRAPHY

"*Preparing for Passover*." Hebrew for Christians. https://www.hebrew4christians. com/Holidays/Spring_Holidays/Pesach/Preparations/preparations.htm.

"*Public Trust in Government: 1958–2022*." June 6, 2022, Pew Research Center. https://www.pewresearch.org/politics/2022/06/06/public-trust-in-government-1958-2022/.

Ream, Norman S. "*Morality in America*." July 1, 1993, Foundation for Economic Education. https://fee.org/articles/morality-in-america/.

"Revolutionary War," History.com. https://www.history.com/topics/ american-revolution/american-revolution-history.

Richter, Sandra L. "*Epic of Eden: Isaiah.*" *September 1, 2019. Seedbed.* https:// my.seedbed.com/product/the-epic-of-eden-isaiah/.

Ritenbaugh, John. "*Prophets and Prophecy.*" Bible Tools. www.Bibletools.org.

Ritenbaugh, John. "Prophets and Prophecy (Part 2)." *Church of the Great God.* www.cgg.org.

Roberts, Alastair. "Rightly Dividing Red Sea.*" Rightly Dividing the Red Sea.* 3 Mar. 2020. www.thegospelcoalition.org.

Ruszala, Michael. "*Two Nations Under God: Israel and America's Foundation.*" Ascension. https://media.ascensionpress.com/2019/07/04/two-nations-god/.

"*SB 7054: Central Bank Digital Currency.*" The Florida Senate. https://www. flsenate.gov/Session/Bill/2023/7054.

Spalding, Matthew, "*The Formation of the Constitution.*" September 14, 2007, The Heritage Foundation. https://www.heritage.org.

"Tevilah: Immersion of Vessels." *Chabad.Org,* www.chabad.org.

"*The Pilgrims' Formula to Save America,*" *from Monumental: In Search of America's National Treasure* video. Directed by Duane Barnhart. Word Films P & D, 2012.

"*The Root Cause of All Sin.*" Messiah-Of-God. www.messiah-of-god.com/root-cause-of-all-sin.html.

Tkach, Joseph. "Jesus Christ: The Unexpected Messiah." *Grace Communion International.* www.gci.org.

Torczyner, Rabbi Mordechai. "*Yehoshua—The Book of Joshua—From Slaves to Israelis,*" *December 26, 2017,* YouTube video. 27:33. https://www.youtube.com/ watch?v=vjlKZJQ4kJo.

Williams, James. "Old Testament Background for Christian Baptism." *Seed and Water for Souls*. www.seedandwater.org.

Winnail, Douglas S. "*Miracles of the American Revolution.*" Tomorrow's World, July-August 2017. https://www.tomorrowsworld.org/magazines/2017/july-august/miracles-of-the-american-revolution.

Winthrop, John. "A Model of Christian Charity" in *A Library of American Literature, Vol. 1, Early Colonial Literature, 1607–1675*. ed. Edmund Clarence Stedman and Ellen Mackay Hutchinson. New York: Charles L. Webster & Company, 1888.

Witherspoon, John. "The Dominion of Providence over the Passions of Men" in *Political Sermons of the American Founding Era: 1730–1805*, ed, Ellis Sandoz. Indianapolis: Liberty Fund, 1990.

Made in the USA
Columbia, SC
12 January 2024

30323564R00055